Plant-Based Juniors Cookbook: Kids-Friendly Plant-Based Recipes For Every Home

Ida Smith

Published by Ida Smith, 2021.

While every precaution has been taken in the preparation of this book, the publisher assumes no responsibility for errors or omissions, or for damages resulting from the use of the information contained herein.

PLANT-BASED JUNIORS COOKBOOK: KIDS-FRIENDLY PLANT-BASED RECIPES FOR EVERY HOME

First edition. September 28, 2021.

ISBN: 979-8201435523

Written by Ida Smith.

Table of Contents

Introduction

One reason people love to switch to a plant-based meal is that it gives you a healthy skin, improves your health, and fills you with a lot of energy. However, while trying to switch to plant-based meals, don't get carried away, you need to be careful not to feed your kids with unhealthy plant-based meals. Make your kids something sweet, healthy and plant-based. If you are already feeling overwhelmed, below are 30 amazing and healthy plant-based recipes to make for your young ones.

Recipe 1 - Spicy baked Zucchini fries

Make plant-based meal fun and exciting for your kids, baked and spicy zucchini fries is a perfect way to spice things up in the kitchen.

Cooking Time: 60 minutes

Yield: 4

Recipes

- 4 pieces of zucchinis
- 1/3 cup of soy milk
- ½ cup of yeast, nutritional
- 2 tsp. of garlic powder
- ½ cup of Italian seasoning
- 1 tbsp. of baking powder
- ½ tsp. of salt
- 1 tbsp. of red chili flakes

Directions

Preheat the oven to about 400°. Line your baking pan with your parchment paper and set aside. Cut off the ends of your zucchini and chop into fries. Place the zucchini in a colander, sprinkle salt on it and keep for about 30 minutes until it sweats.

Drain the fries and dry with a paper towel. Pour your soy milk in a small bowl and set aside. Place your Italian seasoning, baking powder, garlic, yeast, and salt in another bowl and mix properly.

Dip the zucchini fries in the milk, and toss into your seasoning mixture and place in the baking pan. Repeat with all the fries and bake for about 30 minutes. Remove from oven and serve.

Recipe 2 - Vegetable soup

Soups are great for a cold morning and a cold night. You can prepare this vegetable soup to keep your kids warm.

Cooking Time: 30 minutes
Yield: 6
Recipes

- 1/2 cup of alphabet pasta
- 1 tsp. of grapeseed oil
- 1 medium sized well diced yellow onions
- 2 big chopped celery stalks
- 1/2 cup of chopped red bell pepper
- 1 clove of minced garlic
- 1 tsp. of salt

- 1/3 tsp. of allspice, ground
- 4 cups of vegetable stock
- 2 cups of tomato and vegetable juice
- 2 cups of mixed vegetables, frozen
- 1 tbsp. of lemon juice

Directions

Boil a pot of water and add your pasta, and cook until tender. Remove, drain and set aside. Heat your grapeseed oil in a pot, add onion, bell pepper, celery, garlic, and salt and keep stirring while it cooks for about 5 minutes.

Add the allspice, tomato vegetable juice, stock, and mixed veggies and let it boil. Cook partially covered for about 10 minutes. Add your pasta and lemon juice and simmer for a few minutes, remove and serve hot.

Recipe 3 - Fresh corn salsa

Looking for a quick and easy plant-based meal to prepare? You've got one right here. This meal is made with different flavors that keep the kid excited.

Cooking Time: 20 minutes

Serve: 4

Recipes

- 12 ounces of fresh corn
- 2 red deseeded and diced red bell pepper
- 2 pieces of deseeded and sliced jalapeno pepper
- 2 small onions, diced
- 1/2 cup of cilantro, chopped and fresh
- 1 tbsp. of lime juice
- 1 tbsp. of agave nectar

* 1/2 tsp. of salt

Directions

Thaw your corn and place in a bowl, then add your red bell pepper, jalapeno pepper, and onions mix properly, then add your cilantro, juice, nectar, and salt.

Combine properly and let it stand for about 35 minutes so it can absorb all the flavors before serving.

Recipe 4 - Chocolate chip with chickpea

Chocolate chip chickpea cookie with vanilla and peanut butter is not just delicious but also very nutritious.

Cooking Time: 20 minutes
Yield: 20
Recipes

- 1 cup of oats, rolled
- 1 can of rinsed and drained chickpeas
- 8 pitted medjool dates
- ½ cup of peanut butter, creamy
- ½ tbsp. of vanilla
- 1/3 tbsp. of sea salt
- ½ cup of chocolate chips

Directions

Blend your oats until it becomes flour, add your chickpeas, vanilla, peanut butter, dates, and salt in the flour and mix until it becomes sticky.

Add your chocolate chips in it and blend until it is properly incorporated, remove from blender and roll into about 20 balls.

Store in your fridge until it is ready to be eaten.

Recipe 5 - Baked hash brown mushroom

Baked hash brown gives it a crispy texture and they are great to add to the breakfast table.

Cooking Time: 45 minutes

Yield: 4

Recipes

- 10 ounces thawed hash browns, frozen
- 2 tbsp. fresh rosemary, minced
- 1 tbsp. yeast flakes
- 2 tbsp. garlic, minced
- ½ tsp. salt
- ½ tsp. ground black pepper
- 1 medium-sized onion, diced
- 1 bell red pepper, deseeded and sliced
- 10 ounces sliced mushrooms
- ½ cup of vegetable stock

Directions

Preheat your oven to 350 degrees. Line a baking dish with a parchment paper, and set aside. Mix your hash browns with your rosemary, garlic, yeast, salt and pepper in a bowl, mix properly and spread it in your baking pan.

Place in your oven and bake for about 20 minutes or until it is soft and golden brown and crispy. In a pan, add your vegetable stock, simmer and put your onion, mushrooms, and bell pepper in the stock and simmer until it is soft. Add a little salt and pepper to taste.

When your hash brown is done, remove from oven and place in your mushroom pan, toss gently, remove and serve.

Recipe 6 - Nut milk

Do you still buy nut milk in the store? Then it's time to try making some by yourself. Homemade nut milk is everything you want; it is healthy, plant-based and tasty.

Cooking Time: 5 minutes

Yield: 1

Recipes

- 1 cup of almonds, raw
- 3 cups of water
- 2 medjool dates, pitted
- 1 tsp. of vanilla extract
- 1/3 tbsp. of ground cinnamon

Directions

Soak your almonds overnight in cold water, then by morning, discard the water, rinse your nut properly and drain. Blend your nuts in a blender; add your water, dates, extract, and cinnamon. Keep blending until it becomes smooth.

Pour mixture into a clean nut milk bag and strain the solids from the milk, place in a clean jar and chill in your fridge.

Recipe 7 - Grilled cinnamon sandwich

Do you need to prepare a quick plant-based breakfast for your little ones? This is a perfect recipe that is easy to make and saves time as well.

Cooking Time: 25 minutes
Yield: 2
Recipes

- 4 bread slices
- 3 tsp. of natural peanut butter
- ½ tbsp. of raspberry jam
- ½ tsp. of ground cinnamon
- 1 tbsp. of chia seeds
- 1 tsp. of raisins
- ½ tbsp. of vegan butter

Directions

Spread your peanut butter on two slices of bread. Then on the other bread slices, spread your jam on them. Spread your ground cinnamon on the bread slices, add your raisins, and chia seeds, press the bread slices together to make a sandwich.

Heat your vegan butter in a pan, place the sandwiches in it and grill until it becomes golden brown. Turn the other side and grill.

Remove and serve with hot cup or coffee or tea.

Recipe 8 - Eggless pasta dough

Kids love pasta and transforming it into the dough without egg is something you should try. The kids won't even notice it was made without eggs.

Cooking Time: 35 minutes

Yield: 2

Recipes

- 2 tbsp. of oil
- 1 cup of water, warm
- 1 tsp. of tomato paste
- 3 cups of flour
- ½ tsp. of salt

Directions

Mix your oil in warm water in a small bowl, then add your tomato paste in it and whisk properly. Pour your flour and remain a little flour for kneading, then add salt in the flour, place flour on a board and make a well in the middle.

Pour your oil mixture in the hole you made and whisk the flour with a fork bit by bit until it is well mixed. Use your hands to knead for about 5 minutes. Sprinkle your left over flour on the surface and keep kneading.

If your dough seems to hard, add water and knead until smooth. Wrap your dough in a plastic wrap and let it rest for about 20 minutes and set aside. Meanwhile, dust your rolling pin with flour as well as your work surface. Place your dough on the surface and make it rectangular, then use your rolling pin to knead until it is thin like a pasta then cut pasta into the shape you want, place in a pot of salted water and cook for about 5 minutes, then remove and serve with any sauce of your choice.

Recipe 9 - Black bean and tofu burger

Kids love burgers, they prefer to snack on burgers than to eat a real food. To keep them snacking on healthy burgers with this unique recipe.

Cooking Time: 60 minutes

Yield: 4

Recipes

- 1 tbsp. of chia seeds

- ½ cup of water
- 1 cup of tofu, firm, pressed, and drained
- 2 tsp. of soy sauce
- 1 can of drained and rinsed cooked black beans
- ½ cup of chopped and rinsed mushrooms
- 2 tsp. of garlic powder

- 1/3 cup of tomato paste
- ½ tbsp. of smoked paprika
- 1 tbsp. of yeast
- ½ tsp. of salt
- ½ cup of oat flour
- 2 tsp. of oil

Directions

Mix your chia seeds and water in a bowl and set aside, while you keep stirring it. Preheat your oven to about 350° then line your baking pan with parchment paper and set aside. Crumble the tofu in a bowl with your hands and mix your soy sauce together.

Spread the crumbled tofu in your baking pan, add the black beans, and mushrooms and bake for about 20 minutes. Transfer the black beans to a bowl and mash it with a fork. Add the mushroom and tofu to the bowl, and add paprika, garlic, tomato paste, yeast and salt.

Add the chia egg and oat flour to your burger mix, and combine properly, divide mixture into 4 parts and form burger patties, place in a plate, cover and refrigerate for about 30 minutes until it is firm.

Remove from fridge and cook over medium heat for a few minutes and serve.

Recipe 10 - Baked orange flavor apples

If you need an amazing plant-based breakfast for the kids or dessert, this recipe can be perfect for them.

Cooking Time: 50 minutes

Yield: 4

Recipes

- 4 big apples
- 1/3 cup of sucanat
- 1/3 cup of dry oats
- 2 tbsp. of raisins
- ½ tsp. of ground cinnamon
- ½ tsp. of nutmeg, ground
- ½ tsp. of cloves, ground
- 1/3 cup of walnuts, chopped
- 1 tsp. of orange zest

Directions

Preheat your oven to about 350 degrees. Line your baking pan with a parchment paper and set aside. Remove the cores from your apples, then leave a layer of the apple at the bottom. Place apples in your baking pan, then mix your sucanat, cinnamon, oats, cloves, nutmeg, zest, walnuts, and raisins in a bowl.

Divide mixtures among the apples in the pan, place in the oven and bake for about 40 minutes or until the apples are soft. Remove from oven and serve.

Recipe 11 - Oil-free fried rice

Kids love fried rice, but this time, it's going to be oil-free and also kid-friendly. It's a perfect plant-based recipe that is healthy and tasty.

Cooking Time: 45 minutes
Yield: 4
Recipes

- ½ chopped sweet onions
- 2 thinly sliced carrots
- 2 cups of water
- 4 cloves of crushed garlic
- 2 cups of shredded cabbage
- 1 cup of peas, frozen
- 2 cups of brown rice, cooked
- 1 cup of scrambled tofu
- ½ cup of soy sauce

Directions

Add a little water in a pan then add your carrots, garlic, and onions and cook for about 3 minutes while stirring. Then add your cabbage, stir and let it simmer for another 5 minutes. Keep adding water bit by bit when necessary to prevent it from sticking.

Add your frozen peas, brown rice, scrambled tofu, and soy sauce. Keep stirring while it is cooking for another 10 to 15 minutes.

Remove and serve.

Recipe 12 - Coconut flavored blueberry sauce

The coconut-flavored sauce will be perfect for a breakfast of pancakes or French toast. Believe it or not, your kids will lick their fingers.

Cooking Time: 20 minutes

Yield: 4

Recipes

- 2 cups of fresh blueberries
- ½ cup of water
- 1 cup of orange juice
- 1/3 cup of agave nectar
- ½ cup of cornstarch
- ½ tbsp. of coconut flavor
- 1/3 tsp. of ground cinnamon

Directions

Heat a pan and mix your blueberries, a little water, juice, and agave in the pan and stir gently until it boils. Mix your cornstarch and remaining water in a small bowl and pour the cornstarch mixture in the blueberry sauce.

Continue to simmer until it is thick and remove from the heat, add the coconut flavor and cinnamon. If the sauce is too thick, you can add a little water to make it light. Then serve with your French toast or pancakes.

Recipe 13 - Smoky veggie Mac and cheese

Smoky veggie Mac and cheese is oil-free and kid-friendly. It is healthy and very tasty. Your kids will have fun with this snack.

Cooking Time: 40 minutes

Yield: 6

Recipes

- 5 cups of water
- 1 cup of unsalted raw cashew
- 1 tbsp. of yeast
- 1 tbsp. of smoked paprika
- 1 tbsp. of tomato paste
- 2 tsp. of garlic powder
- ½ tbsp. of lemon juice, fresh

- ½ tbsp. of salt
- 1/3 tbsp. of Dijon mustard
- ½ cup of reserved cashew water
- 2 cups of macaroni
- 1/3 cup of vegan butter

Directions

Pour the water in a pot and bring to boil over high heat. Once the water has boiled, add the cashews and salt and cook for about 10 minutes. Remove cashew from water, drain and retain the water,

Place your cashew in a blender, add yeast, tomato paste, paprika, garlic powder, lemon juice, Dijon mustard, salt, vegan butter and your remaining cashew water and blend properly until it is smooth.

Pour the creamy mixture to your macaroni, and then add salt to taste and serve.

Recipe 14 - Wheat fluffy pancakes

These fluffy pancakes are made with whole wheat flour and this is just perfect for your blueberry sauce.

Cooking Time: 15 minutes

Yield: 4

Recipes

- 1 cup of whole wheat flour
- 1 tbsp. of sucanat
- 1 tbsp. of baking powder
- 1/3 tbsp. of salt
- 1 cup of milk, non-dairy
- 3 tbsp. of applesauce, unsweetened

Directions

Mix all your dry ingredients in a bowl and set aside. Then in another bowl, mix your milk and applesauce together and pour the mixture into your dry ingredients and mix properly.

Heat a pan, then drop your batter in the heated pan bit by bit and let it cook until you see the bubbles. Flip the other side and cook for extra few minutes

Repeat until the batter is finished, then remove and serve with your blueberry sauce.

Recipe 15 - Strawberry flavored peanut butter jelly bars

It's a fun time for kids and the peanut butter jelly bar is fun, healthy, tasty, and nutritious.

Cooking Time: 40 minutes

Yield: 6

Recipes

- 2 tbsp. of coconut oil
- 1/2 cup of peanut butter
- 1 flax egg – mixture of flaxseeds and a little water
- 1 tbsp. of coconut sugar
- 2 tbsp. of oat flour - blend
- ½ tbsp. of vanilla extract
- 1/3 cup of strawberries (Fresh)
- 1/3 cup of strawberry jam

- 1 can of natural peanut butter
- ½ can of unsalted peanuts, raw

Directions

Preheat your oven to about 300° and line your baking pan with parchment paper and set aside. Place your oats in a food processor and blend and set aside. In another bowl, mix your flax seed with water and let it set for just few minutes to form a flax egg.

Pour your coconut oil in a big bowl, add the peanut butter, flax egg, and vanilla, stir properly then add your sugar and oat flour and stir properly. Transfer mixture to your baking pan and spread it evenly.

Spread the jam on it, place your fresh strawberries on it and bake for about 30 minutes. Remove from oven and let it cool. Sprinkle your peanut butter on it and the chopped peanuts and serve.

Recipe 16 - Cinnamon and apple cereal

Are your kids transitioning to plant-based meals? Then don't bore them, give them exciting meals like this special cereal.

Cooking Time: 40 minutes
Yield: 4
Recipes

- 1 cup of oats
- 1 cup of milk, non-dairy
- 1 cup of applesauce, unsweetened
- ½ tbsp. of ground cinnamon
- 1/3 tbsp. of ground nutmeg
- 1 big apple, peeled, cored, and diced
- 1/3 cup of sucanat

- 1 cup of warm water
- ½ tsp. of salt
- ½ tbsp. of vanilla extract

Directions

Mix all of the ingredients in a pan and let it simmer on low heat for about 30 minutes or until your oat is soft. Remove from heat and serve with your apples and other types of fruit and serve.

Recipe 17 - Wilted spinach salad

Spinach salad mixed with walnut gives this salad a unique taste. Kids love any meal that is flavored and tasty, so with this, you can never go wrong with your children's meal.

Cooking Time: 15 minutes
Yield: 2
Recipes

- 1 tbsp. of sesame oil
- 1 pack of shiitake mushrooms, stemmed and sliced
- 5 cups of washed and dried baby spinach
- 2 tbsp. of Apple cider vinegar
- 1 cup of chopped walnuts
- 1 clove of minced garlic
- 1 small onion, diced

- 1/2 tsp. of kosher salt
- 1 tbsp. of dijon mustard
- 1/2 cup of oil
- 1/2 tsp. of fresh ground black pepper

Directions

Heat your sesame oil in a pan, add your shiitake and simmer for about 2 minutes. Add your walnuts and garlic and stir for another 2 minutes. Add your onion, salt, dijon mustard, and apple vinegar and let it boil.

Remove from heat and gently add the oil and spinach and mix until it is wilted. Season with a little black pepper and serve.

Recipe 18 - Applesauce cornbread

Cornbread in applesauce has a very sweet taste and is suitable for kids. You can serve it with a nice bowl of salad, Mexican-style preferable.

Cooking Time: 30 minutes

Yield: 6

Recipes

- 2 tsp. of Ener-G egg replacer
- ½ cup of warm water
- 2 cups of cornmeal, finely ground
- 1 tbsp. of baking powder
- ½ tbsp. of salt
- 1 cup of soy milk
- 2 tbsp. of applesauce

- 1/3 cup of agave nectar

Directions

Preheat the oven to 350°. Line a square shaped baking pan with parchment paper and set aside. Mix your egg replacer in a small bowl with water and also set aside. Combine your cornmeal, baking powder, and salt in another bowl, add your soy milk, agave, applesauce, and the egg replacer mixture together and pour mixture into your baking pan and bake.

Bake for about 15 to 20 minutes or if you inserted a toothpick in it, bake until the toothpick comes out with ease. Remove and serve warm.

Recipe 19 - Grilled artichoke chickpeas sandwich

Grilled artichoke hearts will make your kids ask for more, it is easy to make on a very busy day.

Cooking Time: 20 minutes

Yield: 1

Recipes

- 1 can of rinsed and drained chickpeas
- 1 can of marinated grilled and drained artichoke heart, reserve 2 tbsp. of marinade
- 1 tbsp. of rinsed and drained salted capers
- 1 tbsp. of red wine vinegar
- 1 tsp. of dulse flakes
- 4 round whole wheat rolls, crusty and sliced
- 2 big tomatoes, sliced
- 4 romaine lettuce leaves

- 1/2 small onion, diced
- 2 tbsp. of pitted olives, chopped
- 1/3 cup of oil
- 1/2 tsp. of fresh ground black pepper

Directions

Blend your chickpeas, artichoke, and the leftover marinade in your food processor then add the capers, vinegar, and dulse flakes until it reaches a rough puree consistency.

Divide the chick pea mixture into your wheat rolls and top the mixture with your slices of tomato, lettuce, and onions. Sprinkle with olives and oil, season with your black pepper and serve.

Recipe 20 - Baked potato chips

Instead of buying chips from the store, baking it at home is very healthy and delicious.

Cooking Time: 40 minutes

Yield: 4

Recipes

- 4 big sized yellow potatoes
- 1/ tbsp. of salt

Directions

Preheat the oven to about 400°. Line a baking tray with parchment paper and set aside. Clean the potato and cut them in thick slices and ensure the slices are the same size so it will all cook at the same time.

Place the slices in cold water and let it stand for about 25 minutes. Remove from water and drain, pat dry with a paper towel and arrange in your lined baking tray. Sprinkle salt on it and bake for about 2 minutes or until the potatoes is crispy and tender. Keep turning until they are golden brown, remove and serve warm.

Recipe 21 - Creamy tasty guacamole

Guacamole tastes great anytime and any day. You can have it with your chips or on sandwiches for your kids.

Cooking Time: 10 minutes

Yield: 4

Recipes

- 4 ripe potted and peeled avocado
- 3 tbsp. of lime juice
- 1 ripe cored, deseeded, and chopped tomato
- 1 small red onion, diced
- 1/2 cup of fresh cilantro, chopped
- 1 medium sized jalapeno pepper, seed removed and minced
- 1/2 tsp. of ground cumin
- 1/2 tsp. of kosher salt

Directions

Place your avocado in a bowl and mash with a fork, add your lime juice, tomato, onion, cilantro, jalapeno pepper, cumin, and salt and mix properly.

Remove and serve immediately.

Recipe 22 - Garlic flavored roasted chickpeas

Roasted chickpeas are snacks that you can eat without having any guilt because it is purely plant-based. It is filled with flavor and very satisfying, and it is one snack that the young ones will love.

Cooking Time: 70 minutes

Yield: 5

Recipes

- 2 cans of rinsed and drained chickpeas
- ½ tbsp. of garlic powder
- 1 tbsp. of chili powder
- ½ tbsp. of sea salt
- 1/3 cup of lime juice

Directions

Preheat your oven to about 400° and line your baking pan with parchment paper and set aside. Place your chickpeas in a plastic bag that can be sealed, add your garlic, chili, salt, and lime juice in it, shake properly until it is well mixed.

Spread the chickpeas in your baking pan and bake for about 50 minutes. Stir it and bake again for another 15 minutes so it can be well cooked. When it becomes golden brown, remove and serve warm.

Recipe 23 - Buffalo Beans and vegetables

Buffalo beans and veggies is an amazing meal that will give you a wonderful experience. It is tasty and very healthy.

Cooking Time: 35 minutes

Yield: 4

Recipes

- 1 pack of tofu, cubed
- 1 cup of buffalo wing sauce, oil free
- 1 tbsp. of liquid smoke
- 2 bunches of sliced kale and stems removed
- 2 can of pinto beans, drained and rinsed
- 4 cups of brown rice, cooked
- 1 cup of blue cheese dressing

Directions

Preheat the oven to about 350°. Line your baking pan with parchment paper and see aside. Place your tofu in a bowl and add the Buffalo sauce and let it marinade for about 1 hour.

Remove the tofu from the marinade, place in your baking pan, and bake for about 15 minutes or until the edges are dry and brown and ensure you turn over the other side.

Steam your kale in small water until it becomes wilted, drain and place your beans with the kale, mix well until properly coated. When you are ready to serve, place your rice in your serving bowl, then add the kale mixture, and top it with your tofu, sprinkle your blue cheese on it, and serve.

Recipe 24 - Rice salad in a southern style

Rice salad is another healthy plant-based recipe that your young ones will love. It is a healthy meal for the family and it is very rich in vegetables.

Cooking Time: 10 minutes

Yield: 4

Recipes

- 2 cups of already cooked rice, brown
- 1 cup of bell pepper, chopped
- 1 cup of kernel
- 2 cans of black beans
- ½ big avocado, seed removed and diced
- 2 tbsp. of oil
- ½ tsp. of salt

- ½ tsp. of cumin
- ½ tsp. of chili powder

Directions

Place your cooked rice in a bowl, then add all your veggies in it, mix properly. Add your salt, cumin, chili powder, and oil, toss properly until well mixed and serve chilled.

Recipe 25 - Tofu salad without egg

Tofu salad is an interesting replacement of egg salad, you need to try this for your kids and they won
even notice that it is without egg.

Cooking Time: 15 minutes

Yield: 5

Recipes

- 1 can of extra firm tofu, drained and crumbled
- 1/3 cup of green onion, sliced
- 1/3 cup of fennel, well chopped
- 2 tbsp. of cashew mayonnaise
- 2 tsp. of dijon mustard
- 1 tbsp. of lemon juice
- 2 tbsp. of fresh parsley, chopped

- 1 tsp. of curry powder
- 1 tbsp. of dill weed, dried
- 1/3 tsp. of paprika
- 1/2 tsp. of ground cumin
- 1/2 tsp. of salt
- 1/2 tsp. of fresh ground black pepper

Directions

Place tofu in a bowl, add your other ingredients into the same bowl and combine properly. When it is well coated, serve your salad in sandwich or in a wrap and serve.

Recipe 26 - Blueberry and walnut cookies

Muffins are the kids' favorite snacks and making them from plant-based ingredients makes them more healthy and nutritious.

Cooking Time: 30 minutes

Yield: 8

Recipes

- 2 cups of oat flour
- 1/3 tbsp. of baking soda
- 1/3 tbsp. of baking powder
- 1/2 tsp. of salt
- 1/2 cup of non-dairy milk
- 1 tbsp. of lemon juice
- 1/3 cup of oil

- 2 tbsp. of maple syrup
- 1 tsp. of vanilla
- 1 cup of blueberriess
- 1/2 cup of chopped walnuts

Directions

Preheat your oven to 350°. Grease your baking sheet and set aside. Whisk your flour, baking soda, baking powder, and salt in a bowl and set aside. Then in another bowl, mix your milk, lemon juice, oil, maple syrup, and vanilla until is properly mixed.

Add your blueberries and walnuts, then scoop mixture in 8 mounds and place on your baking sheet. Place in the oven and bake for about 15 minutes or until it becomes golden brown.

Remove and serve warm.

Recipe 27 - Jackfruit BBQ

Most vegetarians consider jackfruit to be their meat, however, transforming your green jack fruit into some amazing BBQ will excite the kids and they will love it.

Cooking Time: 7 hours

Yield: 4

Recipes

- 2 cans of green jackfruit drained
- 1 cup of BBQ sauce
- 1 medium sized onion diced
- 1 deseeded and diced green pepper

Directions

Rinse your jackfruit properly, then place in a slow cooker will all your ingredients and let it cook overnight or for about 4 hours. When it begins to fall apart and pull, use a fork and pull it apart from the fruit, and stir properly.

Cook for another 1 hour, remove and serve hot to the kids or let it cool a bit.

Recipe 28 - Avocado lemon pesto

When it comes to pesto on sandwiches or pizza, or even on salads, it tastes great. What makes this recipe unique is the fact that it is made of oil and it is very rich and creamy.

Cooking Time: 10 minutes

Yield: 4

Recipes

- 2 cups of basil, fresh
- 1/3 cup of pine nuts
- 1 tbsp. of lemon juice
- 2 cloves of minced garlic
- 1/2 tsp. of salt
- 2 tbsp. of yeast flakes
- 1/2 tsp. of cayenne pepper
- 1/2 tbsp. of fresh black pepper

- 1 fresh pitted and peeled avocado
- 2 tbsp. of water

Directions

Mix all your ingredients in a food processor and blend until it is smooth. If it has too thick, you can add water to make it lighter. And serve with your sandwich or pizza.

Recipe 29 - Tasty potato salad

Potato salad is a traditional meal that has become popular. The salad is a combination of potato and veggies, which makes it healthy and nutritious for your kids.

Cooking Time: 40 minutes

Yield: 6

Recipes

- 2 pounds of red potatoes
- 4 stalks of celery, sliced thinly
- 1 small red onion cut in half
- 6 sliced green onions
- 1/2 cup of tofu mayonnaise
- 1 tsp. of agave nectar
- 2 tbsp. of Apple cider vinegar

- 2 tsp. of dijon mustard
- 1/2 tbsp. of salt
- 1/2 tsp. of fresh black pepper

Directions

Cut your potatoes in chunks and place in a large pot covered with water. Allow it to boil for about 10 minutes, then with low heat, continue cooking until it is tender. Drain potatoes and rinse with cold water.

Place the potatoes in a bowl and add all your veggies in it, mix gently and properly, and serve.

Recipe 30 - Black bean dip in southwestern style

Black bean dip is spicy and filled with amazing flavors.

Cooking Time: 15 minutes

Yield: 4

Recipes

- 2 cans of rinsed and drained black beans
- 1 tbsp. of minced chipotle
- 2 tbsp. of roasted garlic, smashed
- 1 tsp. of chili powder.
- 1/2 cup of vegetable stock
- 2 tbsp. of roasted diced bell pepper
- 1 tbsp. of chopped cilantro, fresh

Directions

Place all your ingredients in a food processor and blend leaving out the bell pepper and cilantro. When the mixture is smooth, add your cilantro and bell pepper and blend slightly.

Remove from blender and serve.

Conclusion

Kids are usually not friends with plant-based meals because they love to have junks and lots of animal food. But, this cookbook has come to your rescue because it contains 30 unique and exciting kids-friendly recipes that your young ones will love and will not mind having them daily. These recipes are out of this world and it is a must-try for every home.

Don't miss out!

Visit the website below and you can sign up to receive emails whenever Ida Smith publishes a new book. There's no charge and no obligation.

https://books2read.com/r/B-A-LRXL-WSGSB

BOOKS 2 READ

Connecting independent readers to independent writers.

www.ingramcontent.com/pod-product-compliance
Lightning Source LLC
Chambersburg PA
CBHW081301130726
47998CB00010B/2888